THE FIVE SENSES

Smelling

by Lisa Owings

BLASTOFF! READERS
3

BELLWETHER MEDIA • MINNEAPOLIS, MN

Note to Librarians, Teachers, and Parents:

Blastoff! Readers are carefully developed by literacy experts and combine standards-based content with developmentally appropriate text.

Level 1 provides the most support through repetition of high-frequency words, light text, predictable sentence patterns, and strong visual support.

Level 2 offers early readers a bit more challenge through varied simple sentences, increased text load, and less repetition of high-frequency words.

Level 3 advances early-fluent readers toward fluency through increased text and concept load, less reliance on visuals, longer sentences, and more literary language.

Level 4 builds reading stamina by providing more text per page, increased use of punctuation, greater variation in sentence patterns, and increasingly challenging vocabulary.

Level 5 encourages children to move from "learning to read" to "reading to learn" by providing even more text, varied writing styles, and less familiar topics.

Whichever book is right for your reader, Blastoff! Readers are the perfect books to build confidence and encourage a love of reading that will last a lifetime!

This edition first published in 2018 by Bellwether Media, Inc.

No part of this publication may be reproduced in whole or in part without written permission of the publisher. For information regarding permission, write to Bellwether Media, Inc., Attention: Permissions Department, 5357 Penn Avenue South, Minneapolis, MN 55419.

Library of Congress Cataloging-in-Publication Data

Names: Owings, Lisa, author.
Title: Smelling / by Lisa Owings.
Description: Minneapolis, MN : Bellwether Media, Inc., [2018] | Series: Blastoff! Readers. The Five Senses | Includes bibliographical references and index.
Identifiers: LCCN 2017029555 | ISBN 9781626177703 (hardcover : alk. paper) | ISBN 9781618912985 (pbk. : alk. paper) | ISBN 9781681034799 (ebook)
Subjects: LCSH: Smell–Juvenile literature. | Nose–Juvenile literature. | Senses and sensation–Juvenile literature.
Classification: LCC QP458 .O95 2018 | DDC 612.8/6–dc23
LC record available at https://lccn.loc.gov/2017029555

Editor: Rebecca Sabelko   Designer: Lois Stanfield

Printed in the United States of America, North Mankato, MN.

Table of Contents

Around the Campfire

You unzip your tent and step inside. The **musty** smell brings back fun memories.

Later, you help with the campfire. The scent of smoke fills the air.

Your favorite campfire activity is toasting marshmallows. You enjoy the company while you wait for them to cook.

Oh no! What is that burnt smell? Cooking over a fire is hard. But you are having so much fun, it does not matter.

What Is Smelling?

We use our noses to smell everything from yummy food to stinky socks.

All scents come from tiny **molecules** floating through the air.

molecule

molecule

Every time we breathe in,
we draw scent molecules
into the nose.

They hit a special lining at the top of the **nasal cavity**. This slimy lining holds millions of **receptor cells**.

nasal cavity

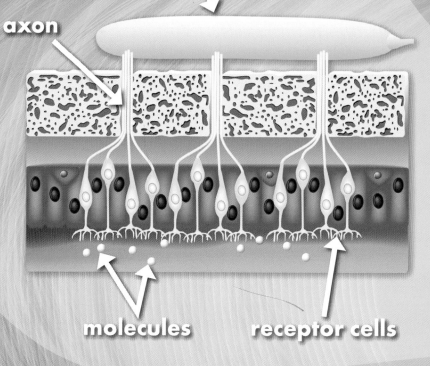

olfactory bulb

axon

molecules

receptor cells

Each receptor cell is shaped so only one type of scent molecule can attach to it. The molecules fit into the cells like keys into locks.

Then, the cells send messages up their **axons** into the brain's **olfactory bulb**.

olfactory bulb

The olfactory bulb **processes** messages about smells. Some messages are sent to other areas of the brain.

messages

That is why smells make us react differently. Some spark memories. Others send us running for safety!

Our noses teach us about food. In fact, smell makes up most of our sense of taste!

Smells that make our mouths water usually mean food is good to eat. If food smells bad, we usually should not eat it.

Our noses are great at warning us of danger. The smell of smoke or gas tells us to act quickly.

People without a sense of smell lose this warning system. They must be extra careful to stay safe.

Smells are strongly connected to memories and feelings. What goes through your mind when you smell sunscreen or freshly baked cookies? Take a deep breath and enjoy your sense of smell!

Sniffing Up Memories

Our sense of smell helps us recall memories.

Gather a few items whose scents might unlock pleasant memories. Not sure what to smell? Try crayons, grass clippings, or a loved pet. Grab a notebook and pen. Then take a moment to smell each item. Write down what memories, feelings, or thoughts come to mind.

- What was your favorite scent?

- What was the most surprising feeling or memory?

Glossary

axons—the long, threadlike tails of nerve cells where messages related to the senses are passed

molecules—the smallest pieces of substances; molecules are too tiny for humans to see.

musty—smelling stale

nasal cavity—the air-filled space behind the nose

olfactory bulb—a part of the brain above the nasal cavity that gathers scent information; receptor cells connect to the olfactory bulb.

processes—prepares, changes, or groups items or facts

receptor cells—cells that react to scents or other things in the outside world; receptor cells send messages about the outside world to the brain.

To Learn More

AT THE LIBRARY

Duhaime, Darla. *Gross Smells.* Vero Beach, Fla.: Rourke Educational Media, 2016.

Lay, Kathryn. *Smelling Their Prey: Animals with an Amazing Sense of Smell.* Minneapolis, Minn.: Magic Wagon, 2013.

Patent, Dorothy Hinshaw. *Super Sniffers: Dog Detectives on the Job.* New York, N.Y.: Bloomsbury, 2014.

ON THE WEB

Learning more about smelling is as easy as 1, 2, 3.

1. Go to www.factsurfer.com.

2. Enter "smelling" into the search box.

3. Click the "Surf" button and you will see a list of related web sites.

With factsurfer.com, finding more information is just a click away.

Index

The images in this book are reproduced through the courtesy of: Asia Images Group, Cover; Logra, pp. 4-5 (tent); dugdax, pp. 4-5 (background); Soloviova Lludmyla, pp. 5, 6-7, 7; Goran Bogicevic, p. 8-9; Andrey_Popov, pp. 9, 18-19, 19; molekuul_be, p. 9 (molecule); Wxin, p. 10-11; ibreakstock, p. 10 (molecule); Teguh Mujiono, pp. 11, 13, 13 (brain), 14, 14 (brain); Designua, p. 12; Pressmaster, p. 15; Zurijeta, pp. 16-17; Peter Bernik, p. 17 (top); Iakov Fillimonov, p. 17 (bottom); Jack Frog, p. 20; CookiesForDevo, p. 21 (top); Ifaritovna, p. 21 (middle); archimede, p. 21 (bottom).